U.S. HISTORY IN REVIEW

The Great Depression

Emmett Martin

Enslow Publishing

Please visit our website, www.enslow.com. For a free color catalog of all our high-quality books, call toll free 1-800-398-2504 or fax 1-877-980-4454.

Portions of this work were originally authored by John O'Mara and published as *The Great Depression*. All new material this edition authored by Emmett Martin.

Cataloging-in-Publication Data
Names: Martin, Emmett.
Title: The Great Depression / Emmett Martin.
Description: Buffalo, NY : Enslow Publishing, 2027. | Series: U.S. History in review | Includes glossary.
Identifiers: ISBN 9781978547100 (pbk.) | ISBN 9781978547117 (library bound) | ISBN 9781978547124 (ebook)
Subjects: LCSH: Depressions–1929–Juvenile literature. | Depressions–1929–United States–Juvenile literature. | United States–Economic conditions–1918-1945–Juvenile literature.
Classification: LCC HB3717 1929.M327 2027 | DDC 330.9730916–dc23

Published in 2027 by
Enslow Publishing
2544 Clinton Street
Buffalo, NY 14224

Designer: Leslie Taylor
Interior layout: Tanya Dellaccio Keeney
Editor: Therese Shea

Photo credits: Series art (grunge flag) Andrey Kuzmin/Shutterstock.com; series art (stamp icon) Stocker_team/Shutterstock.com; series art (font) santstock/Shutterstock.com; series art (swash) BUTENKOV ALEKSEI/Shutterstock.com; cover (main), pp. 19, 29 Everett Collection/Shutterstock.com; p. 5 Standret/Shutterstock.com; p. 7 Studio Romantic/Shutterstock.com; p. 9 Jonathan Weiss/Shutterstock.com; p. 11 (top) MikeDotta/Shutterstock.com; p. 11 (bottom) Lucky-photographer/Shutterstock.com; p. 12 https://upload.wikimedia.org/wikipedia/commons/6/68/Argonaut_Oil_%26_Mining_Co_stock_1900_and_rev_stamps.jpg; p. 13 Thapana_Studio/Shutterstock.com; p. 15 (top) https://upload.wikimedia.org/wikipedia/commons/e/e1/Crowd_outside_nyse.jpg; p. 15 (bottom) https://upload.wikimedia.org/wikipedia/commons/f/f2/19291030_Crash_of_%2729_-_New_York_Times.jpg; p. 17 (top) https://upload.wikimedia.org/wikipedia/commons/6/67/Bank_of_the_United_States_failure_NYWTS.jpg; p. 17 (bottom) https://upload.wikimedia.org/wikipedia/commons/c/cc/American_union_bank.gif; p. 21 https://upload.wikimedia.org/wikipedia/commons/a/ac/Schoolchildren_line_up_for_free_issue_of_soup_and_a_slice_of_bread_in_the_Depression%2C_Belmore_North_Public_School%2C_Sydney%2C_2_August_1934_-_Sam_Hood_%283550268287%29.jpg; p. 23 (top) https://upload.wikimedia.org/wikipedia/commons/9/97/Hooverville_on_the_Seattle_tideflats%2C_1933_%2850495168952%29.jpg; p. 23 (bottom) https://upload.wikimedia.org/wikipedia/commons/5/57/President_Hoover_portrait.jpg; p. 25 https://upload.wikimedia.org/wikipedia/commons/f/fd/FDR-1944-Campaign-Portrait_%283x4_retouched%2C_cropped%29.jpg; p. 27 https://upload.wikimedia.org/wikipedia/commons/e/ef/SocialSecurityposter1.gif.

Printed in the United States of America

CPSIA compliance information: Batch #CSENS27: For further information, contact Enslow Publishing, New York, New York, at 1-800-398-2504.

Contents

It's All About Money 4
Good or Bad? 6
From Recession to Depression 8
Soaring Stocks 10
The Crash 14
Banks Fail 16
From Bad to Worse 18
Trying to Survive 20
Shantytowns 22
Enter FDR 24
New Deal Programs 26
Economic Recovery 28
A Timeline of the Great Depression 30
Glossary 31
For More Information 32
Index 32

*Words in the glossary appear in **bold** the first time they are used in the text.*

It's All About Money

Talk about the economy sounds **complicated** on the news. But there's a simple way to explain it. An economy is all the ways people make and use money. People make money and spend it in many, many different ways.

Learn More

The economy has to do with how people make, sell, and buy goods and services. Goods are objects people buy, such as cars. Services are actions people pay for, such as car repairs.

Good or Bad?

Economies are sometimes **described** as good or bad. In a good economy, there are many high-paying jobs, businesses make money, and people spend money. In a bad economy, people lose jobs and businesses close. People have less money. If this happens for at least 6 months, it's called a recession.

Learn More

A person who studies the economy and the many parts of it is called an economist.

From Recession to Depression

If a recession becomes worse, the economy is said to be in a depression. Many more people across a country lose jobs. More businesses fail. Banks fail too. A famous depression in U.S. history began in 1929. It's called the Great Depression.

Learn More

A recession or depression can happen for many reasons, such as wars or too many or too few goods being made.

Soaring Stocks

The years before the Great Depression were called the Roaring Twenties. It was a time of much economic growth in the United States. Many people grew richer by buying stocks. Stocks are shares in a company's ownership. As a company's success grows, the price of its stock goes up.

the New York Stock Exchange

Learn More

The buying and selling of stocks and **bonds** is called a stock exchange, or stock market. A stock exchange is also where buying and selling happens, such as the New York Stock Exchange.

In the 1920s, stock prices rose because people wanted more stocks. However, other parts of the economy weren't doing well. More people lost jobs. People had less money. Prices of goods fell. But people bought stocks because they hoped they could sell them for more money.

stock certificate, 1900

Learn More

Today, you can track online how the value of a company's stock goes up and down every day.

online stock trading

The Crash

In September 1929, stock prices began to fall sharply. People hurried to sell stocks before they lost more value. On October 24, 1929, around 13 million shares of stock were sold. This began the stock market crash.

On October 29, 1929, more than 16 million shares of stock were sold at the New York Stock Exchange. This was called Black Tuesday.

STOCKS COLLAPSE IN 16,410,030-SHARE DAY, BUT RALLY AT CLOSE CHEERS BROKERS; BANKERS OPTIMISTIC, TO CONTINUE AID

LEADERS SEE FEAR WANING

Point to 'Lifting Spells' in Trading as Sign of Buying Activity.

GROUP MEETS TWICE IN DAY

But Resources Are Unable to Stem Selling Tide—Lamont Reassures Investors.

HOPE SEEN IN MARGIN CUTS

Banks Reduce Requirements to 25 Per Cent—Sentiment in Wall St. More Cheerful.

Resources of the banking group which was organized last Thursday to stabilize conditions [illegible] market were utilized [illegible] break the force of the [illegible] of selling which acco[illegible] biggest day, from the [illegible]

240 Issues Lose $15,894,818,894 in Month; Slump in Full Exchange List Vastly Larger

The drastic effects of Wall Street's October bear market is shown by valuation tables prepared last night by THE NEW YORK TIMES, which place the decline in the market value of 240 representative issues on the New York Stock Exchange at $15,894,818,894 during the period from Oct. 1 to yesterday's closing. Since there are 1,279 issues listed on the New York Stock Exchange, the total depreciation for the month is estimated at between two and three times the loss for the 240 issues covered by THE TIMES table.

Among the losses of the various groups comprising the 240 stocks in THE TIMES valuation table were the following:

Group.	Number of Stocks.	Decline in Value.
Railroads	25	$1,128,686,488
Public utilities	29	5,135,734,327
Motors	15	1,689,840,902
Oils	22	1,332,617,775
Coppers	13	824,403,820
Chemicals	9	1,621,697,897

The official figures of the New York Stock Exchange showed that the total market value of its listed securities on Oct. 1 was $87,073,630,423. The decline in the 240 representative issues therefore cut more than one-sixth from the total value of the listed securities. Most of this loss was inflicted by the wholesale liquidation of the last week.

U. S. STEEL TO PAY

RESERVE BOARD FINDS

CLOSING RALLY VIGOROUS

Leading Issues Regain From 4 to 14 Points in 15 Minutes.

INVESTMENT TRUSTS BUY

Large Blocks Thrown on Market at Opening Start Third Break of Week.

BIG TRADERS HARDEST HIT

Bankers Believe Liquidation Now Has Run Its Course and Advise Purchases.

Stock prices virtually collapsed yesterday, swept downward with gigan[illegible] in the most disastrous trad[illegible] in the stock market's his[illegible] of dollars in open mar[illegible] were wiped out as prices [illegible]

New York Times article, 1929

Banks Fail

People became **panicked**. They tried to take all their money out of banks. Many banks didn't have enough money on hand for everyone. They had used money for **loans** and **investments**. About 9,000 U.S. banks failed by 1933.

Learn More

During the Great Depression, people didn't have the money to pay back loans from the bank. This added to more banks failing.

From Bad to Worse

The bad parts of the economy made things worse for other parts of the economy. People had less money, so they bought fewer goods. Businesses slowed **production** or shut down. More people lost jobs. Those with jobs earned less. By 1933, 15 million Americans were out of work.

Learn More

In the 1930s, **droughts** and dust storms hit the Great Plains. Farms couldn't grow enough crops. Millions moved, but couldn't find new jobs.

dust storm, 1935

Trying to Survive

Millions of Americans became very poor during the Great Depression. People lost their homes. Whole families went hungry. Those who had nothing to eat stood in long lines for free bread, soup, and other foods. Some people who had been millionaires sold apples on the streets.

Learn More

The United States began to buy fewer goods from other countries and loaned less money. The Great Depression soon spread to other nations.

Shantytowns

Many who became homeless built shelters out of things they could find. These homes made from cardboard, glass, wood, and tin were called shanties. Sometimes thousands lived in camps called shantytowns. These communities were unhealthy and at times unsafe, but people had no place else to go.

Learn More

Some blamed President Herbert Hoover for the Great Depression. They called shantytowns Hoovervilles.

Herbert Hoover

Enter FDR

Hoover's **federal** government didn't act strongly to stop the depression or help U.S. citizens. Hoover wanted local governments and **charities** to help people. In 1933, Franklin D. Roosevelt became U.S. president. He began a group of **programs** called the New Deal to fight the Great Depression.

Learn More

Roosevelt, also called FDR, ordered banks to close until the government was certain they wouldn't fail.

New Deal Programs

New Deal programs provided millions of jobs. The Civilian Conservation Corps (CCC) put people to work planting trees. The Public Works Administration (PWA) hired workers to build bridges and dams. The Works Progress Administration (WPA) built roads, schools, and airports.

Learn More

The Social Security Act was another part of the New Deal. It provided a **pension** for older people and those who were **disabled**.

Economic Recovery

The U.S. economy slowly got better during the New Deal years. Many people were still out of work, though. In 1941, the United States entered **World War II**. People got jobs in factories preparing for the war. Others joined the armed forces. The Great Depression came to an end.

Learn More

While the United States has had recessions, it hasn't had another depression. The federal government often acts when the economy begins to do badly.

A Timeline of the Great Depression

1929
The stock market crashes in October.

1930
Banks begin to fail.

1931
Droughts and dust storms in the Great Plains cause crops to fail.

1932
Franklin D. Roosevelt is elected president.

1933
Roosevelt orders banks to close for a time.

1934
The Securities and Exchange Commission (SEC) begins to watch over stock market activities.

1935
The Social Security Act is passed, helping the elderly and disabled. Other New Deal programs put people to work.

1939
World War II begins.

1941
The United States enters World War II.

Glossary

bond: A paper that shows a government or company promises to pay back borrowed money with interest, or more money.

charity: An organization that helps people in need.

complicated: Having many parts which are hard to understand.

describe: To say what something is like.

disabled: Being unable to do some of the tasks of daily life.

drought: A long period of very dry weather.

federal: Having to do with the national government.

investment: Something someone buys hoping it will increase in value.

loan: Money given to someone that must be paid back.

panic: To feel sudden, uncontrollable fear.

pension: Money paid by a company or government to someone old or sick who no longer works.

production: The action of making or growing something to sell it.

program: A plan of things done in order to get a certain result.

World War II: The global conflict from 1939 to 1945 in which many countries fought.

For More Information

Books

Kenney, Karen Latchana. *The Great Depression.* Minneapolis, MN: Bearport Publishing, 2024.

Stout, Tim. *The Great Depression: From Hard Times to the New Deal.* New York, NY: First Second, 2025.

Website

U.S. History: The Great Depression
www.ducksters.com/history/us_1900s/great_depression.php
Read more about how the Great Depression changed the nation.

Publisher's note to educators and parents: *Our editors have carefully reviewed these websites to ensure that they are suitable for students. Many websites change frequently, however, and we cannot guarantee that a site's future contents will continue to meet our high standards of quality and educational value. Be advised that students should be closely supervised whenever they access the internet.*

Index

banks, 8, 16, 17, 25, 30
Black Tuesday, 15
businesses, 6, 8, 18
Great Plains, 19, 30
Hoover, Herbert, 23, 24
Hoovervilles, 23
jobs, 6, 8, 12, 18, 19, 26, 28
New Deal, 24, 26, 27, 28, 30
recession, 6, 8, 9, 29
Roaring Twenties, 10
Roosevelt, Franklin D., 24, 25, 30
shanties, 22
stock market crash, 14, 30
stocks, 10, 11, 12, 13, 14, 15
World War II, 28, 30